Hunter Hayes

ABDO
Publishing Company

Big
Buddy BOOKS
Buddy Bios

by Sarah Tieck

VISIT US AT
www.abdopublishing.com

Published by ABDO Publishing Company, PO Box 398166, Minneapolis, Minnesota 55439.

Printed in the United States of America, North Mankato, Minnesota.
102013
012014

 PRINTED ON RECYCLED PAPER

Coordinating Series Editor: Rochelle Baltzer
Contributing Editors: Marcia Zappa, Megan M. Gunderson
Graphic Design: Maria Hosley
Cover Photograph: *AP Photo*: Jordan Strauss/Invision.
Interior Photographs/Illustrations: *AP Photo*: Evan Agostini/Invision (p. 7), Mark Humphrey (p. 11), Donn Jones/
    Invision (p. 19), Chris Pizzello/Invision (p. 19), Matt Sayles (p. 11), Charles Sykes/Invision (p. 23); *Getty
    Images*: Mark Davis/ACMA2012 (p. 5), Mark Davis/ACMA2013/Getty Images for ACM (p. 11), Rick Diamond/
    ACMA2012/Getty Images for ACM (p. 17), Rick Diamond/ACMA2013/Getty Images for ACM (p. 27), Matthew
    Eisman (p. 25), Tyler Golden/NBC/NBCU Photo Bank via Getty Images (p. 29), Adriane Jaeckle (p. 9), Chris
    Polk/ACM2013/Getty Images for ACM (p. 21), Stephen Saks (p. 7), Donna Svennevik/ABC via Getty Images
    (p. 15), Paul Warner (p. 13); *Shutterstock*: spirit of america (p. 13).

Library of Congress Cataloging-in-Publication Data

Tieck, Sarah, 1976-
  Hunter Hayes : country singing sensation / Sarah Tieck.
    pages cm. -- (Big buddy biographies)
  ISBN 978-1-62403-199-1
1. Hayes, Hunter, 1991---Juvenile literature. 2. Country musicians--United States--Biography--Juvenile literature. I.
Title.
  ML3930.H35T54 2014
  782.421642092--dc23
  [B]
                                2013029174

Hunter
Hayes

Contents

Rising Star

Hunter Hayes is a country singer. He has released albums and popular songs. He has even won awards!

Hunter is well known. He has appeared on magazine covers. And, he has been interviewed on popular television shows.

Hunter sings and plays many instruments, including the guitar.

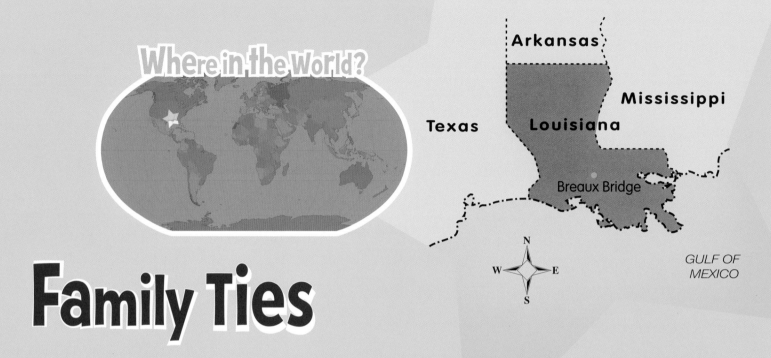

Where in the World?

Arkansas

Mississippi

Texas   Louisiana

Breaux Bridge

N
W   E
S

GULF OF
MEXICO

Family Ties

Hunter Easton Hayes was born in Breaux Bridge, Louisiana, on September 9, 1991. His parents are Lynette and Leo Hayes. He has no brothers or sisters.

Hunter grew up listening to **Cajun** music. His family often ate at a local restaurant with live music. Young Hunter began picking up objects and playing them like instruments. Soon, he started teaching himself to play real instruments.

Breaux Bridge is known as a place to eat crawfish. It is also known for its Cajun music.

Hunter began attending music shows and events at a young age. Now, he attends even more as a country star!

First Steps

Hunter enjoyed singing from a very young age. He wanted to be a **professional** country singer. So, he worked hard to learn skills. He played instruments, sang for others, and worked to be a better **performer**.

At age four, Hunter started playing with a local band. In 2000, he **released** his first album. It is called *Through My Eyes*. A year later, he released *Make a Wish*.

8

As a child, Hunter played the accordion.

Country Legends

Country music stars noticed Hunter's talent. They asked him to **perform** with them. Hunter was excited to work with famous singers. They taught him about life as a musician.

In 1997, Hunter sang "Jambalaya" with Hank Williams Jr. There is even a video on YouTube of Hunter and Hank singing.

Hunter has played music with country stars Johnny Cash and June Carter Cash.

Hunter also performs with modern country stars, such as Brad Paisley (*center*) and Dierks Bentley (*right*).

Building a Career

As a teenager, Hunter played music often. He was very focused on growing his musical skills. Hunter's family supported his dream. They built a **studio** in their house. In 2008, they moved to Nashville, Tennessee. There, Hunter became a **professional** songwriter.

Hunter finished high school by taking classes at home. That way, he could focus on his music.

Nashville is known for country music. Many famous singers got their start there.

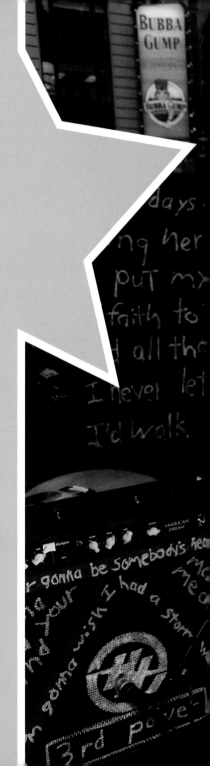

Talented Singer

After finishing high school, Hunter began writing and recording more songs. Around this time, he made an album called *Songs About Nothing*. He wanted to show record companies what he could do. He hoped they would notice his work.

Hunter writes his own songs. He wrote his first one at age six! He gets ideas from listening to many different artists.

Big Break

In 2011, Hunter **released** his first major album. It is called *Hunter Hayes*. The album has many different styles of songs. Some are slow with lots of feeling. Others have a strong beat.

The album has several popular songs. "Wanted" became a number one country hit. And, "Storm Warning" sold so many copies it became a Gold Single. Other popular songs include "Love Makes Me" and "Somebody's Heartbreak."

In 2012, Hunter toured with Carrie Underwood. He was her opening act!

Award Winner

Hunter's singing and songwriting have earned him honors. In 2012, he was named as a possible winner of three **Grammy Awards**. He was up for the Best New Artist, Best Country Solo **Performance**, and Best Country Album awards.

Also that year, Hunter won the New Artist of the Year award from the Country Music Association (CMA). And, he earned a Teen Choice Award for Choice Male Country Artist.

As part of his work, Hunter does live radio interviews.

Off the Stage

Even in his free time, Hunter enjoys working on his music. He also spends time with friends and family. And, he would like to learn to fly airplanes.

Hunter also likes to help others. In 2013, he **performed** at the Academy of Country Music's Party for a Cause.

Party for a Cause helped raise money to fight hunger and help military groups.

Buzz

Hunter's opportunities are growing. He continues **performing** his music in concerts and on television. Fans are excited for more music from Hunter Hayes!

In June 2013, Hunter performed on *The Voice*.

Snapshot

★**Name**: Hunter Easton Hayes

★**Birthday**: September 9, 1991

★**Birthplace**: Breaux Bridge, Louisiana

★**Albums**: *Through My Eyes, Make a Wish, Songs About Nothing, Hunter Hayes, Hunter Hayes (Encore)*

Important Words

Cajun of or relating to a group of people from southern Louisiana with French roots. Cajun ways of life include folk music and spicy food.

Grammy Award any of the awards given each year by the National Academy of Recording Arts and Sciences. Grammy Awards honor the year's best accomplishments in music.

interview to ask someone a series of questions.

perform to do something in front of an audience. A performance is the act of doing something, such as singing or acting, in front of an audience.

professional (pruh-FEHSH-nuhl) working for money rather than only for pleasure.

promote to help something become known.

release to make available to the public.

studio a place where music is recorded.

Web Sites

To learn more about Hunter Hayes, visit ABDO Publishing Company online. Web sites about Hunter Hayes are featured on our Book Links page. These links are routinely monitored and updated to provide the most current information available.

www.abdopublishing.com

31

Index